The Adventures of Mr Harry C

Written and Illustrated By

Anissa Papadakos

Copyright

© 2018 Magic Walls & Canvas. All rights reserved.

ISBN: 978-0-6484-235-0-8

All rights reserved. No part of this publication may be reproduced or transmitted in any form or by any means, electronic or mechanical, including photocopying, recording, storage in an information retrieval system, or otherwise, without the prior written permission of the publisher, unless specifically permitted under the Australian Copyright ACT 1968 as amended.

Dedication

This book is lovingly dedicated to Peter, Oriana & Marcela

for their endless stream of love

And to my one and only Ivana

Acknowledgements

Anything is possible when you have the support of beautiful and amazing people.

Big thank you to my amazing husband Peter, who never stops believing in me and in my dreams. You are one in a million and I am very lucky to have you in my life.

Big thank you to my best friends Oriana and Marcela, who have always been there for me and who have supported me no matter what. Your friendship and love means the world to me.

Big thank you to Rachel. You are a beautiful soul and I am so grateful for all your help and support throughout this journey.

Last but not least, big thank you to my family and friends for all your support.

Meet Mr Harry C, our friendly neighbourhood Cupid.

He is sad because he lost his glasses and can't see.

Oh my, how will Mr C do his job of spreading love in the world.

Mr Harry C decided to retrace his footsteps, hoping he could remember where he left his glasses.

He went to see Elly the Elephant at the Zoo.

"Hi Elly, how are you?"

"Have you seen my glasses?"

"Hi Mr C, no sorry I haven't seen your glasses"

With tears in his eyes, Mr Harry C went to see Old Nana.

She always had an answer to everything.

Sadly, this time she didn't know where Harry could have left his glasses.

But being the nice old lady that she was, she let Harry borrow hers.

Finally Mr Harry C could see.

He was so happy and very excited as he could now continue to spread love all over the world.

"Oh No", said Mr C. "I can't remember where I have left my bow and arrows".

"What am I going to do?".

Mr Harry C decided to go seek the help of Wendy the witch.

Wendy was the neighbourhood's friendliest witch, she lived in a big scary house on Crones Street.

Even though she had a great big wart on the end of a great big nose, she also had a heart of gold.

Mr Harry C knocked on Wendy the witch's door.

KNOCK, KNOCK, KNOCK.

The door opened, "Why Mr C, what a pleasant surprise".

"How can I help you?", said Wendy.

Harry explained what had happened and asked Wendy for her help.

"Of course I will help you Mr C!".

"Let's jump on my broom and we will go ZOOM, ZOOM, ZOOM".

Their first stop was into space to visit the Man in the Moon.

Maybe he knows where Mr C's bow and arrows are?

"I have never been into space", said Harry.

"You will love it Mr C", cackled the witch.

"Are you ready? One, Two, Three".

Off they flew.

Higher and higher they sped towards the Moon.

Quick as a flash they arrived on the Moon.

It was a magical place with lots of rocks, sparkling stars and plenty of room.

Wendy the witch decided to lead the way; they walked and walked and eventually found their way.

There he was, as tall as can be, sat no other than Mr Moony.

Mr C said, "Man in the moon we have travelled a long way, do you know where my bow and arrows are?"

In a deep voice Moony replied, "No I don't know where they are". "Perhaps your best bet is to ask Saint Nicky, he is a star".

They gave thanks to the Man in the Moon and quickly jumped back on their broom.

The next destination was the North Pole.

Hopefully Big Nick could help the mystery unfold.

They were welcomed in by Nick himself and Harry C gave a shout.

"Oh please Mr Nicky surely you know what has happened to my bow and arrows?"

"Harry my dear I have no idea".

"But to help you on your quest, please take my sleigh and I wish you all the best".

They really thought Mr Nicky could solve their mystery, but to no avail Mr C felt like he had failed.

"Don't be upset Mr C", yelled Wendy.

"We have Mr Nicky's sleigh, so let's at once set upon our way".

"But where do we go?", asked Harry.

With a shrug Wendy said, "Let's head towards home and see what else the day will hold".

They travelled in silence and deep in thought.

Thinking and wondering that the bow and arrows must be near.

Surely they just can't disappear.

High amongst the clouds they went when Wendy suddenly yelled, "Look Mr C there is a cluster of colours, a rainbow it must be".

"Let's fly down and ask Mr Lenny the Leprechaun, surely he knows where your bow and arrows have gone?"

And there, as cool as can be, sat none other than Mr Lenny, "Well hello my dear friends, how do you do?"

"How can I help you?"

Mr Harry C said, "My dear Lenny I am not sure if you have heard, we have travelled the world".

"Up and down, here and there, zimming, zooming everywhere".

"But to no avail, my bow and arrows are nowhere".

Suddenly Mr C went quiet and started to cry.

Wendy the witch spoke up and said, "Lenny be a dear, do you know where Harry's bow and arrows have disappeared?"

Lenny jumped off his mushroom and said, "When things go amiss, the one place it could be is at home! Let's go and see".

Wendy and Mr Harry got so excited.

Why of course let's go back to where it all had started.

They zimmed and zoomed as quick as can be.

No time to stop, no siree!

Suddenly the sleigh came to a holt, just outside Harry's loft.

He ran inside looking here and there but could not find his bow and arrows anywhere……

"Oh Mr Cupid", said a little voice.

"It's your good friend Sally, from down the road".

"I have something to tell you, so please be quick".

"Pop over, let's talk and share some cake and tea".

Mr Harry C floated down to Earth ever so gently.

"Oh my dear Sally, how do you do?"

"I would love to have some tea with you".

"Yay", said Sally with lots of joy.

"But before we start I thought you might know that I have found your bow and arrows; here you go".

Harry looked at Sally with a start.

"My dear Girl I can't believe it".

"How did this happen? Oh please tell me I need to hear it".

"I found them in the tree, they must have fallen down from Cloud City".

"In the bird's nest they landed".

"They were guarded and protected, as you can see".

"Mrs Bird knocked on my door and as soon as I saw them I thought OH NO!"

They sat together and sipped tea; all happy, warm and fuzzy.

The sun was shining and the cakes were sweet; all around them you could feel there was a BIG relief.

"My dear Sally thank you for the tea but I must go at once; surely you can see".

"Now that my bow and arrows are safe in my hands, I need to keep spreading love all around".

With his final words he gave a nod, took a leap and off he shot.

"Oh Mr C", said Sally.

"I didn't get the chance to ask, but those are Nana's glasses; where are yours dare I ask?"

As you have noticed we are not yet through, the story will continue to unfold for you.

The one question you may now ask is, "who is the culprit who took Mr C's glasses?"

I have the answer, yes I do, but I am sorry I cannot tell you.

Instead I hope you return for more as the next adventure won't be a bore.

But before we part, I leave you with a clue to who the culprit is that needs to be unmasked-

"What is red, small, and very cheeky?"

www.ingramcontent.com/pod-product-compliance
Lightning Source LLC
Chambersburg PA
CBHW042142290426
44110CB00002B/91